YEAR-ROUND PAPER CRAFTS

YEAR-ROUND PAPER CRAFTS

Celebrate the seasons with hand-crafted cards, tags, decorations and more

Leslie Carola

ARENA BOOKS ASSOCIATES, LLC

An Arena Books Associates Book
www.arenabks.com

Book concept, development, text: Leslie Carola, Arena Books Associates, LLC
Design: Elizabeth Johnsboen, Johnsboen Design
Photography: Jon Van Gorder Studio, Inc.
Copy Editor: Deborah Teipel Zindell

Projects: Judy Ritchie (www.greatamericanstampstore.com),
Susan Swan (www.susanswan.com),
Jamie Kilmartin (www.greatamericanstampstore.com),
Irene Seifer (www.greatamericanstampstore.com), Susan Sheppard,
Jan Williams, Robert Carola, Anastasia Bosakowski-Chater, Leslie Carola
(www.arenabks.com). Individual projects are credited on page.

ISBN: 978-0-9797922-4-3

CONTENTS

INTRODUCTION

Susan Swan

ach season has its own song. And each song has its own rhythm, texture, and color. Crafting through the seasons is a natural. We've responded to the year-round crafting idea with paper crafts abounding with energy, rhythm, and color. Of course, each season has its own holidays—cause for celebration with handmade cards, decorations, and gifts. Keep those seasonal colors, shapes, textures, and rhythms in mind as you plan your projects. Make a list to help you remember.

YEAR-ROUND PAPER CRAFTS offers dozens of ways to transform simple sheets of paper into dazzling, dimensional one-of-a-kind artwork. The fun in doing so is contagious. A simple recipe for success in creating any paper craft

project is to choose a color scheme, create a balanced composition with a focal point, and add some embellishments. The embellishments can be as simple as a mat or two of coordinating colors or a single ribbon, or as complex as multiple layers of folded papers, ribbons, or any number of decorative accents. Techniques include, among others, stamping, cut-paper, piecing paper, punching, accordion folding, tea-bag folding, iris folding, quilling, and layering. And projects include, cards, tags, Easter eggs, Christmas tree ornaments, packages, and tabletop decorations.

Paper is an extraordinary medium. It is versatile, inexpensive, easily stored, even reusable. And who can resist fold-ing, twisting, cutting, punching, piecing, piercing, stitching, weaving, or layering, not to mention coloring, such malleable mate-rial? Experiment to find the papers that you like best to work with, and the ones that re-spond to your hands and touch.

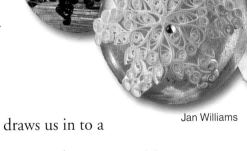

Jan Williams

We respond to color emotionally; it is what draws us in to a project immediately. Reds and yellows—the warm colors—are exciting,

7

while blues and greens—the cool colors—are calming. The most popular coloring agents for paper crafters are colored pencils; dye, pigment, chalk, pearlescent, and alcohol inks; and watercolors. And colored paper, solid or patterned, is magical. The variations are amazing. But don't forget the possibility of making your own colored paper, either with paint or ink, or on your computer in a software program like Adobe Photoshop. You can change size, color, and details with the touch of a button.

Nathalie Métivier

Details make a difference. Dimensional embellishments bring artwork to a whole new level. Cut, punched, and layered shapes create texture and depth. Lift some papers off the surface with foam mounting tape and you have textured layers of increased dimension. Or try rolling a layer of paper to add dimension, like the Winter Flowers example above. Each flower is composed of three stamped, silhouetted, and layered flowers, with the petals of the middle

flower tightly rolled to accentuate the height and dimension of each completed flower. Folding techniques not only add dimension and distinction to a project, they engage one's imagination and sense of joy. There is something irrepressibly appealing about a folded segment that unwinds, or a surprise component that pops up when you open a card. Our aim is to inspire creative thinking. You *can* make the projects exactly as we have, but our hope is that you will take these projects as inspiration to create in your own style.

Robert Carola

Crafting is about celebrating life—the past, the present, and the future. We are making connections to the people, places, and things around us. Whether a quiet one- or two-piece arrangement on a card, or a raucous, elaborate, fun-filled melange with many elements and techniques, let your artwork speak for you. And have fun.

SPRING

We think much of the spring season is cause for celebration. Of course, there are the holidays—St. Patrick's Day, Easter, and Mother's Day, and we certainly observe those, but the season itself is cause for rejoicing. Warmer air, more intense light, new growth in the soil and trees all point to brighter days ahead. So we celebrate all, from the changes in weather, to the delight in a child's eye as he learns a new word, the adoption of a new pet, or the savoring of a long friendship. Crafting is about sharing the small moments in life as well as the major milestones. Life is meant to be shared.

*S*oft, subtle color and a refined patterned paper from which small leaf and blossom shapes have been punched support a stunning botanical arrangement. Large punched and layered flower petal shapes of varying sizes and hues of pink are completed by a spirelli embellishment, a form of string art popular in Europe in which soft thread is woven around and between the petals of a punched flower, skipping a set number of petals to create interesting patterns. The soft pink metallic Kreinik threads wrapped around and between the petals in this project create an appealing texture and a strong focal point. The spirelli pattern for the smaller wreath of thread at the center skips five petals; the pattern for the larger thread wreath behind it skips seven petals.

IRENE SEIFER

IRENE SEIFER

[Above] Pyramid paper-craft art from the Netherlands offers sets of several sizes of progressively smaller decorated precut shapes which you can adhere to a card or page. Remove the five or six pieces of the precut design from the pyramid sheet and adhere them to a prepared surface starting with a base of the largest shape and layering the successively smaller sizes. Pop the art with small pieces of foam mounting tape between each layer. The resulting three-dimensional construction creates intriguing stepped shadows and texture. This octagon shape requires straight, centered layering for the textured pyramid effect.

Nothing says St. Patrick's Day more than leprechauns and shamrocks! The jaunty fellow, below left, can dance a jig or two. Try your hand at creating your own dancing leprechaun using the template on page 118. Cut the shapes out of colored paper, and construct the figure using a pieced paper or cut-paper quilting technique adhering the cut-paper pieces in place on your copy of the drawing. Make the figure in several sizes to use on cards, tags, place cards, or napkin rings, even on magnets or coasters. Fold dark green cardstock to make this 3½ x 5-inch card. Construct the leprechaun from cut, or pieced, paper on white cardstock to fit comfortably on the card front.

Join us for St. Patrick's Day!

ROBERT CAROLA

14

JUDY RITCHIE

[Above] The all-green card features a small glass shamrock ornament on a panel centered on dark green ridged cardstock with a lighter green gingham ribbon woven along the border of the larger panel. The green and white ribbon provides an energetic border. The design is simple, the palette just as simple, and the effect delightful. Texture is what counts here. A Mrs. Grossman's sticker—the small leprechaun and shamrock—on the square decorates a hand-crafted magnet at the left.

NATHALIE MÉTIVIER

[Above] A sunny pastel-colored Easter invitation, place cards, napkin ring, and other table décor welcome all to the festivities of an Easter table.

[Above, left] *Cut 5-inch pale yellow cardstock squares into two triangle shapes.* [Above, right] *Stamp the Bunny image with olive pastel fluid chalk ink at the center of the yellow triangle cardstock. Stamp a second time on scrap paper, and silhouette the image to make a mask.*

[Above, left] *Place the mask directly over the Bunny stamped on the yellow cardstock triangle. Stamp the flowers image on either side of the mask, overlapping the mask on each side. The row of flowers will appear to be behind the stamped Bunny.* [Above, right] *Color the stamped images with fine-quality colored pencils. Embellish with Glossy Accents and Stickles.*

Quilling, or paper filigree, is the art of rolling long, narrow strips of paper around either a needle-like or slotted tool into coiled shapes that are arranged to form decorative designs. Nearly all quilling is done with just a few variations of basic rolls and scrolls. Quilled designs can be featured on cards, tags, or any kind of paper craft, as well as boxes, glass Christmas tree ornaments, or even on these extraordinary quail eggs that have been blown and colored with pigment inks. The quilled flowers add delicate texture and luscious color. The place cards at left show a quick way to create charming table accessories by gluing tiny quilled quail eggs to folded cardstock. The colorful basket, opposite, makes a stunning table arrangement. See page 119 for some basic quilled shapes.

JAN WILLIAMS

JAN WILLIAMS

$\mathcal{E}$ aster eggs extraordinaire! The large colored quilled goose eggs make a handsome Easter table centerpiece or sideboard decoration. The basket of vibrant pink and yellow eggs, at left, with quilled marquise- and crescent-shaped flowers and leaves adds a lighthearted note to an Easter table or any festive celebration. The eggs are blown, colored with pigment ink pads, and embellished with the quilled blossoms and leaves. See page 119 for some basic quilled shape instructions.

JAN WILLIAMS

20

[Above] The solo nested blue egg is adorned with blue and green quilled roses, the directions for which are on page 118. A few marquise-shaped quilled leaves are interspersed with the roses. See page 119 for some basic quilled shape instructions.

JUDY RITCHIE

(Above) The quiet, classically simple centered design of each of these cards is appropriate for Mother's Day, birthday, or any occasion you wish to celebrate. A punched leaf-patterned vase, at left, contains stamped branches and tiny punched flowers. The featured oblong panel is layered on a complementary brown cardstock mat and then on a soft green card. The pink and white palette of the card at right, and the pink and green of the card at back remind us that summer can't be far away.

22

A sensuous palette and a layered, pyramid image in a distinctive and unusual arrangement contribute to a lovely Mother's Day card. The six panels to layer are provided in a set of pyramid cards from Ecstasy Crafts. Remove each panel from the sheet supplied and arrange them in graduated size order. Adhere the largest panel to a burgundy cardstock mat using tape or a glue stick. Continue mounting the next largest panel on top of the previous one using foam mounting tape to lift the panel from the surface. Match the illustration areas to keep the design consistent. Be sure to place a piece of foam mounting tape directly in the middle of each panel to maintain a flat, even surface. These panels are layered at an angle, almost like a fan, to create interesting shadows and a sense of movement. Layering them straight will give a more traditional look.

IRENE SEIFER

[Above, left] Using the template on page 120, cut the frame from violet cardstock. Cut a plain frame shape (without butterflies) from fuschia origami paper. Place the fuschia paper frame on the wood frame under the violet cardstock frame. *[Above, right]* Punch the petals out of pink and light blue cardstock, and fuschia origami paper.

[Above, left] Pop each layer with small pieces of foam mounting tape. Before adhering the violet cardstock layer to the fuschia covered frame, rim the butterfly shapes with flocking powder for a soft, velvety finish. Glue along the edge of each butterfly and, while the glue is still wet, shake on the flocking powder. Silhouette the wings and lift them from the frame surface, leaving the butterfly body attached to the cardstock. *[Above, right]* Adhere the dimensional punched flowers on the top left corner of the frame.

ANASTASIA BOSAKOWSKI-CHATER

[Above] An unfinished wood frame bought, embellished, and filled with a photograph from a cherished trip to Italy provides a special Mother's Day gift. To create exotic dimensional flowers, layer the punched shapes, alternating colors and petal shapes, separating, "popping," each layer with small pieces of foam mounting tape.

[Above] A simple origami-folded vase provides a soft dimensional container for punched and layered spring flowers—ideal for Mother's Day or any spring greeting.

[Above, left] Using the template on page 120, fold a vase from a 3-inch square of patterned paper. [Above, right] Punch three green, two dark pink, and one light pink petal shape using the large Petite Petals punch from McGill. Punch three small yellow suns to serve as the flower centers.

[Above, left] Layer the light and dark pink flowers, alternating the petal shapes and colors. Adhere the layers with a glue pen. [Above, right] Adhere the origami-folded vase at the bottom center of the card, leaving a border at the bottom edge. Adhere the layered blossoms and green leaf swirls on the ivory panel. Layer the decorated ivory panel onto successively larger pink and green mats and then onto the ivory card. Finish with a punched mini yellow sun at the center of each blossom.

[Above, left] Cut white cardstock to 6 x 12 inches. Cut with the grain for ease in folding the card. Fold the left and right outer edges to meet at the center of the card, creating a gatefold. Flatten the creases with a bone folder. [Above, right] Cut decorative paper to a 5¾-inch square. Cut the 5¾-inch square in half to two 2⅞ x 5¾-inch panels. Attach the panels to each side of the card front.

[Above, left] Color three chipboard birds and wings with opposite colors of pigment ink. Start with the lighter colors and build up to the darker tones. Add contrasting tone and texture by increasing the pressure on the pencil as you color. Attach a wing to each bird. [Above, right] Finish the birds with white Peel Off's dots and flower shapes. Cut decorative paper to fit the card interior. Add a colored chipboard bird inside the card. Attach one colored bird to each side of the gatefold opening. Tuck the card edges under the birds.

NATHALIE MÉTIVIER

[Above] An intriguing package enhances the pleasure of gift-giving and gift-receiving. This handsome center gatefold card is held closed by two colorful chipboard birds. Another chipboard bird nestles in the imaginative embellishment on the package itself.

29

An elegant accordion-folded anniversary card filled with memorable, nostalgic photos in vintage sepia tones sets the mood for a romantic remembrance. What a remarkable gift from a daughter for her parents. To create such a meaningful card, gather and scan photos of the individuals and their favorite haunts or journeys. Accordion fold cardstock, adding extra panels as necessary. Some simple collage materials add texture and a bit of color. The focus on texture and a soft palette continues with the vellum envelope and the closure folded from a copy of an interior photograph. The handmade envelope, with gently torn edges, is closed with a simple origami triangular pocket. The envelope closure fold is on page 120. A few tiny punched shapes add a delicate note.

SUSAN SWAN

SUSAN SWAN

JUDY RITCHIE

[Above] Elegance can be so simple. The unadorned stamped images offer pleasing centered compositions with strong focal points and layered messages. The greeting on the card at front is printed on a piece of window plastic and anchored with brass brads at the four corners. The greeting on the card at back is also on a separate panel, stapled at an angle to the simple stamped card.

The cards below speak mainly about texture; dimensional glittering jeweled embellishments decorate the cards at left and rear and the ruffled, quilled blossom on the center panel of the gatefold card in front. The materials available today offer limitless possibilities for mixing techniques. The five pink glass flowers dance above the stamped flower stems. The glittery blue blossoms balance on their stamped stems, and a single quilled blossom and leaves sit prettily on a simple matted panel.

JUDY RITCHIE

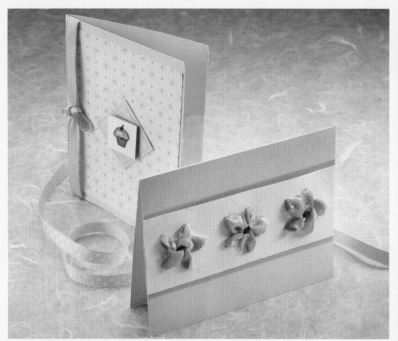

SUMMER

Much of the summer seems like a long holiday with carefree days, time for friends and family, sharing dreams. It is a wonderful time to celebrate, to spend time together, and to create paper crafts. We have designed cards to celebrate large and small moments in our lives, some charming boxes for informal gatherings, gifts, and tabletop decorations with a variety of techniques ranging from stamping; several kinds of folding—including, among others, iris folding, accordion folding, and tea-bag folding; quilling; embroidery; ribbon embroidery; and cut and layered paper. Try something new.

A bouquet of quilled roses—yellow, white, and pink—
presented with punched green leaves and a single bow
of yellow, white, and pink ribbons adorns a summery
June calendar page. See the quilled rose instructions on page 118.

IRENE SEIFER

JUDY RITCHIE

[Above] Three delightful boxes designed to hold gift cards or small gift items are constructed from smooth cardstock with a slot at the top to hold their own gift tags. The box template is on page 121. The gift tags can be any shape you want, as long as they fit in the slot. A ribbon threaded through two holes punched in the upright wings of the top slot adds a playful note. And, of course, you can use any number of techniques to create the gift tags—stamping and embossing, cutting and folding, or punching. Experiment and have fun.

37

The card cover, opposite, is adapted from the cover of a vintage book of fairy tales. Adhere the featured photograph at the center of the card right interior. Create an iris-folded mat using the template on page 118, and layer it over the mounted photograph. (Adjust the size of the mat to the card.) Cut decorative paper to line the whole interior, approximately ½ inch smaller than the open card—to leave a ¼-inch border of card all around the decorative paper liner. To create the two windows, draw appropriate-sized rectangles on the interior liner paper and on the card front. Be sure that all the windows are aligned. Create an attractive finish for the window openings, by cutting an X diagonally from inside corner to inside corner of the drawn rectangle on the liner paper. Fold each triangle of the X back over the straight edge of the window frame, tucked to the back for the interior windows, but pulled through the front window to wrap onto the card front creating an interesting window frame. The multi layers add a distinctive touch.

SUSAN SWAN

SUSAN SWAN

[Above] A striking Father's Day card combines the look of an altered book with a subtle-toned iris-folded mat for a tender photograph of a beautiful child seen through a window cut in the card front.

SUSAN SWAN

40

ather's Day gift cards and gifts can be warm reminders throughout the year of how much Dad is thought of and loved. The gift-wrapped note cards (opposite) will remind a father who travels often to send his own notes home, maybe even with a photograph. Wrap a narrow band of corrugated tan cardboard around a selection of note cards. Attach a small collaged metal panel with decorative brass brads. Add a third brass brad on the other side of the band to create an attractive closure with natural fiber string. Cut the band opening on a diagonal with decorative-edged scissors. The bookmark, right, has a series of meaningful mini ornaments on sturdy ribbon hanging from an embellished square. The long "Happy Father's Day" tag rests on the saved page while the square with dangling ornaments rests on the book cover.

SUSAN SWAN

41

The red, white, and blue palette of most July 4th celebrations resounds with energy. These stocky red star picnic-table candles begged for some patriotic dressing up. Quilled flowers made with five marquise-shaped blue petals accented with tiny red gems are paired two-by-two on a heavy cotton binding tape tied around the middle of each candle. More tiny red gems separate the flowers.

JAN WILLIAMS

JUDY RITCHIE

Above] The trio of red, white, and blue cards extends the palette and the decorative stars and stripes. Texture is a significant element of each one of the cards. The layered panel of three stars rests on a ribbon layer and a textured cardstock surface. The striped sail on the red card is cut from a wide ribbon and layered on the card. The punched red and white stars rest on embossed squares on the card in the foreground.

A stepped accordion-folded card with a charming beach pail, shovel, and sand castle punched along the top edge offers a special invitation to a birthday beach party. Cut paper to 12 x 6 inches. Score at 4-inch intervals along the 12-inch side. Cut the top diagonally as shown, with heights ranging from 6 inches at the left scaling down to 4 inches at the right. Accordion fold and unfold vertically where scored to create three 4-inch-wide panels. Starting at the bottom of the triangle, punch the beach scene edger twice along the top edge of each of the three panels of the card. Using a craft knife, trim the ¼ inch of unpunched paper left between the panels.

Join us at
Jennings Beach
For John's
5th birthday party
Bring tools for a
Sand Castle Contest.
Tuesday, July 8
12:00 p.m.

Party!

JUDY RITCHIE

44

LESLIE CAROLA

[Above] A strong palette and simple shapes are the focus of this easy invitation with a one-layer Diamond Fold tea-bag-folded pattern. Tea-bag folding, originating in the Netherlands, is the art of folding shapes from small squares of paper to assemble in a dimensional motif. Fold the eight Diamond Fold tea-bag shapes, four of each color, following the folding instructions on page 121. For a more complex version create multi layers with a staggered arrangement of shapes.

LESLIE CAROLA

[Above] *Whirling pinwheels have long been a favorite summertime staple. They are easy to make and provide cheerful tabletop accessories. Use the template on page 122 to make the pinwheels. We wanted some size variations so we worked with 4-, 5-, and 6-inch squares of paper printed on two sides.*

46

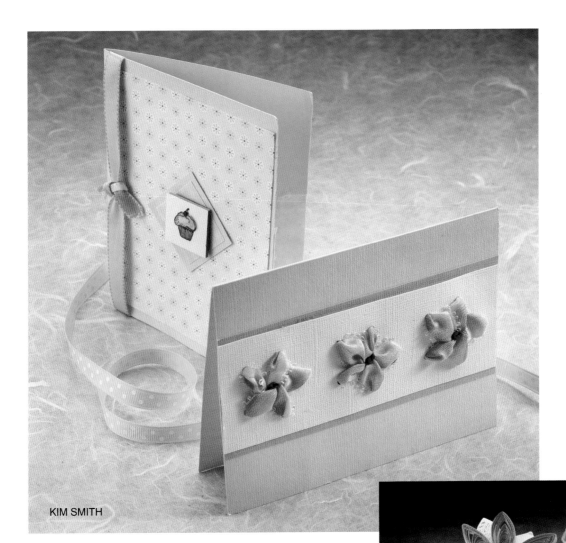

KIM SMITH

[Above] Summery pink ribbon creates three dimensional flowers for a timeless card (foreground). Using an embroidery needle, bring the ribbon up from the back of the white cardstock panel from the outside edge of the flower and stitch down at the center. Pinch each of the five petals of the flowers to add dimension. Layered papers and a stamped cupcake are featured on the card at back. [Right] The quilled flower embellishment is centerstage on the small place card box (holding a luscious chocolate).

JAN WILLIAMS

A charmingly imaginative series of chargers for an al fresco lunch or supper table are created with leaf shapes cut from bright printed paper. You can use any number of printed papers to suit your whim or theme—the possibilities are many. We chose a summer blue and white daisy pattern for this project. Use the leaf shapes template on page 122 to cut leaves of varying shapes and sizes. Cut several of each shape. Create a wreath larger than the plate you will be using. Layer the leaves in a wreath pattern as shown, with much of the pattern visible beyond the rim of the plate. A supporting plate, awaiting a basket of bread, might be tucked *under* the wreath while a dinner plate sits *on top* of the wreath. The leaf place card, opposite, completes the picture.

SUSAN SWAN

SHIRLEY

SUSAN SWAN

*Summery white daisies on a blue field offer
an appealing base for a casual lunch or
supper plate. Change the color of the paper
for a seasonal change.*

49

[Above, left] For the decorative sash: cut black and ivory cardstock to the appropriate heights. For our 13-inch package we cut the black cardstock to 4 inches in height and the ivory to 4½ inches. [Above, right] Stamp an allover pattern in frost white pigment ink on the black cardstock. Color the diamond shapes of the pattern as well as the space between the shapes.

[Above, left] Cut blue Mulberry paper to approximately 6½ inches in height, enough to leave a substantial border above and below the stamped panel to be layered on top of it. Accordion fold the Mulberry paper to form a base. [Above, right] Adhere the stamped cardstock panel to the ivory panel, leaving a narrow ivory border top and bottom and adhere this to the folded Mulberry paper and then to the tissue-wrapped gift. Embellish the wrapped package with additional stamped, cut, colored, and silhouetted images for an attractive flourish.

NATHALIE MÉTIVIER

[Above] This summery light package is wrapped in several layers of bright blue and yellow tissue paper and then layered with a wide dramatic layered sash. The sash panel is rolled around the tissue-wrapped gift, and secured at the back.

51

NATHALIE MÉTIVIER

*A*n inexpensive glass vase, opposite, can be decorated simply with Peel Off's from Magenta and permanent ink markers to become a one-of-a-kind, personal design. A lovely winding path of flowers and leaves embellishes a tall, slim vase. Transferring the Peel Off's shapes is easily done with a tweezers or by gathering the shapes with Magenta's Magic Tape. At right, a simple Flip-Top folded bag made with the template on page 122 in a summery yellow color makes a lovely giftwrap—ideal for any spring greeting. The stamped panel on the bag front is colored to complement the blue and white ribbon.

JUDY RITCHIE

SUSAN SWAN

[Above] A bevy of bright colored cut-paper letters dance across the surface of a festive gift tag, right. The colorful shapes leap from the dramatic black background with resounding energy. Each letter is created by piecing two or three different papers, above at left, overlapping each letter segment. Change the color of the background to change the mood. Change the papers with the change of season. The pieced-paper technique is easy and adaptable. The festive floral papers used are Susan's own creations.

54

A dimensional wreath of tea-bag folded shapes in a modified Star Square Fold catches the light and shadows in a sculptural form. See the template on page123. Tuck the sides of the last folded sections of the top square front behind itself, creating a triangle on the top layer of the folded square. To add more dimension at the center of each triangle insert a thin pencil or awl below the top layer and lift gently. The serene soft green and white palette, the sculptural, almost wind-blown, kite shapes, and the gold bees sing summer's song.

IRENE SEIFER

Ribbon-embroidered yellow roses at the center of an embossed flower shape add an elegant note. Create an embroidery grid similar to the template on page 123 by piercing five- or seven-point (it must be an odd number) star shaped grids on cardstock and stitching with embroidery floss. Stitch from each point of the star in to the center of the figure. Create the ribbon rose by anchoring the ribbon at the center of the rose and winding it alternately over and under each stitched arm of the star. Add the greenery with embroidery floss stitches. Layered mats and a small ribbon bow are lovely finishing touches.

IRENE SEIFER

IRENE SEIFER

[Above] A simple, stylish embroidered flower arrangement and an enchanting, lighthearted purse card are guaranteed to make you smile. The smart little purse is made with a snippet of wide summery plaid ribbon and decorated with yellow flower gems. The flower petals of the card in front are stitched directly on to a white cardstock panel and then matted and layered onto the card, all in shades of peach and green. Simple palettes, strong focal points, and layered, centered, compositions create an appealing effect.

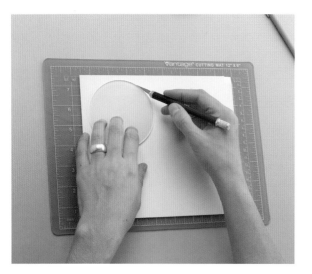 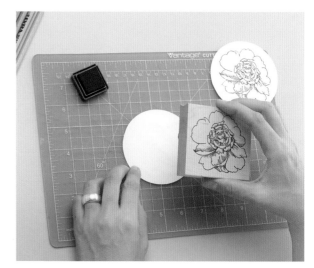

[Above, left] Trace the shape of the coaster onto white cardstock. [Above, right] Stamp the image with black pigment ink on the cut circle.

[Above, left] Color the stamped peony image with several shades of pink/rose colored pencils. Be sure to use good quality colored pencils with a soft core for smooth blending and shading. Balance the color with firmer or lighter pressure on the pencils as you work. [Above, right] Place double-sided adhesive cut to size on the colored artwork. Place the coaster (cloudy side down if there is one) on top of the covered artwork. Apply firm pressure to the layered coaster to remove any air bubbles.

LESLIE CAROLA

[Above] Handmade coasters are an imaginative, inexpensive gift as well as a thoughtful party accessory. The decorative images for these acrylic circle-shaped coasters are easily and inexpensively changed for any occasion. For a summertime gathering, stamp a large single peony shape on a circle cut to the size of the coaster. Color the image, and attach it to the back of the coaster.

Menu
Butternut Squash Soup

Turkey
Chestnut Stuffing
Gravy
Spiral Ham
Candied Yams
Cranberry Sauce
Asparagus
Mashed Potatoes
Green Bean Casserole
Cornbread

Pumpkin Pie
Apple Pie

You're a Hoot!

FALL

Warm fall colors beckon—lots of yellows, oranges, and deep reds—perhaps to combat the cooler mornings and evenings. We nestle indoors to prepare for the festive holidays ahead—Halloween and Thanksgiving, and begin to plan for Chanukah, Christmas, and New Year's. Crafting is at its height at this time of year. Supplies of papers, ribbons, and embellishments of all kinds stimulate inventive crafting ideas.

NATHALIE MÉTIVIER

Dinner reception
Immediately following the ceremony

The Old Manor
12 Romantic Drive
Secret Island

Invitation

ME
2121

Kindly reply
by the twenty first of June

M

Number of persons

[Above] A strong, simple palette, patterned layers, and romantic swirls add up to an interesting ensemble of invitation and various table decorations for wedding festivities. The wedding invitation has a copper-patterned paper sleeve wrapped around the left side of a white card, like an old-fashioned three-piece binding on a book.

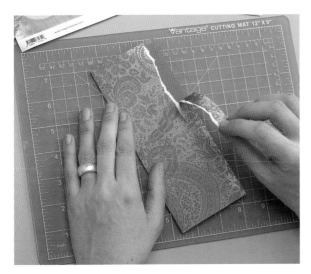 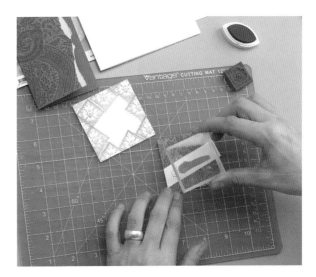

[Above, left] Tear the right edge of the sleeve vertically approximately ½ inch in from its right side. Move the strip slightly to the right (to reveal the torn edge) and attach the sleeve and strip to the white card. [Above, right] Stamp a small pattern in diagonal rows on a white cardstock panel. Stamp the word "Invitation" diagonally across another white cardstock panel. Layer the panels.

[Above, left] Place a flower Peel Off's sticker on a piece of the same decorative paper used in step 1. Silhouette the mounted flower shape. Layer twice for additional texture, slightly rotating the top layer to reveal the petals of both layers. Stamp and silhouette a small flower shape. Cut between the petals of the stamped flower and lift every other petal for added texture. Adhere this to a small circle of another decorative paper of a contrasting color, and attach to the card as shown. [Above, right] Add Peel Off's swirls and dots to the card.

It doesn't take much to turn a commercially purchased item into something very personal and meaningful. A small Bazill Basics Paper 3¼ by 3¾-inch picture frame is embellished with a punched paper flower pot adorned in the lower right corner with a punched and quilled flower in warm rust and yellow fall tones. The decorations are just right for a memorable snapshot of this engaging little boy and his Mom on his first day of pre-school—a big step for all!

JANET WILLIAMS

64

SUSAN SWAN

[Above] A CD of music or images made just for the recipient is a lovely gift at any time of year. This one has an artfully decorated cover —a collage of layered punched shapes, music scores, a date of October 3 on the postcard and the numeral 3 woven in to the collage. Make the cover as personal as you like. The collage format itself allows great freedom in the selection of shapes, colors, texture, and design. Decide before you start what is the purpose for the gift. How do you want the recipient to feel when he or she receives it? Are you celebrating an event, a milestone, or just keeping in touch? A bit of forethought will help keep you and your artwork focused.

65

A simple album cover is a clever invitation to revisit a memorable collection of Halloween celebrations through the years with a family of growing children—siblings, cousins, nieces and nephews. What a thoughtful gathering of whimsical, high-energy moments to be savored by all members of the family. Layered textured cardstock panels, complete with a dangling spider and a handwritten "eeek," adorn the front. A medley of seasonally colored ribbons tied informally at the spine embellish with style.

JAMIE KILMARTIN

JAMIE KILMARTIN

[Above] An elegant trio of pumpkins punched from orange cardstock create a handsome centerpiece for a Halloween table. Punch several (eight or more) oval shapes with decorative edges. For the tall pumpkin at left, fold the punched oval shapes in half vertically; fold horizontally for the smaller, fatter pumpkins. Glue each side of each punched pumpkin to the side of another punched piece. Leave an unglued spot at the top of each pumpkin to insert a stem of rolled green cardstock. Flatten the bottom edge by trimming. Stand the pumpkin on end on a table, plate, or mat. A practical tip to help you use your tools efficiently: the tall pumpkin and the larger rounder one were made with the same punch, but folded differently.

JAN WILLIAMS

Holiday-appropriate decorative layers bedeck a generous-sized gift bag, opposite (obviously for an optimistic trick-or-treater). A layer of Maruyama ribbon running down the front of the bag, to the right of center, is layered with a strip of pumpkin patterned paper on a black mat. Three rectangles of black cardstock at a rakish angle are also layered with Maruyama ribbon and an arrangement of quilled pumpkins and punched leaves. An orange brad secures a punched leaf and each panel to the neighboring one and to the bag itself. The result is playful, festive, and fun. The delightful notebook binder clips, at right, feature a punched and quill-embellished white ghost looking more scared than scary, and a turkey with multicolored feathers. Simple, thoughtful, imaginative gifts for the youngsters in your life.

JAN WILLIAMS

*S*imple, strong, single graphic images—a white ghost on black and silver and a black cat on white and orange on a black bag—dominate their respective bags, one a trick-or-treat bag begging to be filled, and the other a party favor from a Halloween gathering. The clean black and white images are delightfully spooky. Try your hand at drawing your own figures, or use stickers or rubber stamps for the featured icon. The cat and ghost place cards (at left) use the same shapes in a smaller size. The "Boo" party favor boxes are stamped, punched, and decorated with tiny ghost brads. A length of black mesh ribbon slips through the loops at the top of the boxes.

ROBERT CAROLA

basic Halloween palette is easy—black, white, and orange, but it's fun to add another color or two to the mix for added interest. A blue-cloaked, off-beat monster cut from colored paper and attached to the front of a small tan shopping bag looks as though he's out for a night of fun. (I don't think he needs any more sugar, though!) Use the template on page 123 to cut the shapes of the figure. Layer the cut shapes of the head, body, and limbs. Add the eyes and mouth. Use your imagination. Create your monster with his own palette, and his own distinctive features. And make him any size he wants!

ROBERT CAROLA

JUDY RITCHIE

[Above] A clear acrylic bucket is decorated with black spider and spider web stickers, perfect embellishments for a Halloween "bag." Sheer black ribbons at the side are intertwined with narrow orange braided thread. A simple orange circular mat supports the main stickered "Trick or Treat" greeting atop the bucket. The small, round orange and white polka-dot-ribbon-wrapped clear acrylic container of candy corn is not only an attractive and appropriate Halloween party favor; it is also simple to create. Punch the eyes, nose, and mouth from black cardstock and glue to the container front.

73

[Above] Halloween is fun; it brings out the goblin in many of us! A haunted house, with cobwebs, bats, a full moon, and the seemingly resident dog and cat dressed for the evening's treat-seeking events pop up when this card is opened. The three simple stand-up braces are ready to support the three stamped, silhouetted pop-up figures—dog, house, and cat.

Giant stamped spider webs add detail to each corner of the card, opposite. A subdued, but traditional Halloween palette is featured. Cut and fold the card using the template on page 124 to create the braces to support the pop-out features. Adjust the position of the braces to accommodate your design. The pop-out braces and the stamped webs and message are on a liner paper adhered to the inside of the card. More embellished Halloween projects, right, add to the festive evening. Punched and layered orange cardstock ovals form tiny pumpkins to embellish place cards and a gft tag with decorative dimension. Multi layers of printed paper and a die-cut pumpkin add a cheerful note to a trick-or-treat bag. Color and texture reign.

JUDY RITCHIE

75

An appealing trio of black cat cards, right, couldn't be much simpler. The strong graphic image is centered on a white cardstock panel on the pink and rust-colored cards, and positioned on the right edge of a gray panel on the black card. The centered composition of the first two cards is pleasing, but the off-centered composition of the last card adds rhythm and movement. A simple card, below, with the addition of a warm plum tone to the traditional Halloween black, white, and orange colors extends the palette and the pleasure. The two pumpkin brad embellishments are cleverly used as "o's" in the featured word "Boo" at the center of the card front. A special feature of this card is the unexpected Halloween word search game tucked into a pocket inside the card. The word search games can be downloaded from the Internet.

JUDY RITCHIE

JUDY RITCHIE

JUDY RITCHIE

[Above] Cheerful stamped and colored owls, mice, and pumpkins are featured on these two fanciful cards. The sunny palette of the featured panels would be suitable for any season, while the card itself and embellishments say Halloween with humor.

[Above, left] Cut a circle measuring approximately 8 inches in diameter from two Maruyama papers—one red and one yellow. Center the layered circles over the jar lid and secure with a rubber band. Tie a ribbon over the rubber band. [Above, right] Cut a piece of decorative paper long enough to wrap around and cover the height of the jar. Wrap the paper around the jar and glue it at the ends.

[Above, left] Stamp an appropriate image—we chose a large apple and maroon ink—on decorative paper. We used a cling stamp (an unmounted stamp) on an acrylic block, which makes it easy to see the placement of the stamped image. Enhance with colored pencils. Glue the label to the jar. [Above, right] Attach a tag-shaped sticker to a small panel of decorative paper. Accent with colored pencils. Trim the tag, leaving $\frac{1}{8}$-inch border around the sticker shape. Attach a paper flower and leaf with a brad. Attach to the decorated lid.

NATHALIE MÉTIVIER

[Above] Certain items speak volumes about a season, and jars of homemade preserves somehow say autumn. Ordinary commercial jars can be dressed up with Maruyama ribbon, bright-colored, patterned paper labels, ribbons, Peel Off's stickers, and gift tags.

SUSAN SWAN

[Above] Red, purple, and green paper and a large yellow tag holding free-form cut-paper letter shapes create a charming package. Shapes are cut, pieced, and layered to create the individual letters. Susan designed the paper of small colorful circles on a bright red field on her computer in Adobe Photoshop.

xperiment with varying sizes when using the turkey template on page 126. We have made three different cards with three different-sized turkey images, background colors, and embellishments. The turkey is a strong graphic design, the palette is bold, and the compositions simple—an unbeatable combination.

ROBERT CAROLA

agical Thanksgiving tabletop decorations include imaginative, whimsical, individual pie-shaped place cards (perhaps the guest's favorite?), complete with white tissue paper dollops of whipped cream or latticed piecrust. The whipped cream mound is formed by placing a pencil, eraser side down, in the center of a tissue paper square. Pull all of the paper up, crushing it against the sides of the pencil. Repeat for a total of three dollops. Flatten the bottoms slightly and glue to the pie. The punched leaves on the mat visually anchor the place card. The tri-colored, triple-layered, free-standing menu card in the photograph opposite, is covered with three colors of autumnal leaves. The bottom edges of the layers of the menu fold back and are glued together to create support for a standing base, as well as a graceful accent. The folded top edges are graceful.

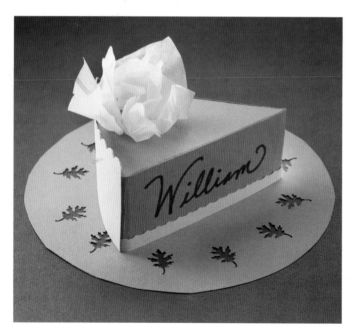

ANASTASIA BOSAKOWSKI-CHATER

Menu
Butternut Squash Soup

Turkey
Chestnut Stuffing
Gravy
Spiral Ham
Candied Yams
Cranberry Sauce
Asparagus
Mashed Potatoes
Green Bean Casserole
Cornbread

Pumpkin Pie
Apple Pie

ANASTASIA BOSAKOWSKI-CHATER

83

WINTER

*H*olidays in the winter months are joyous occasions calling for special handmade cards, decorations, and gifts. Some crafters start early preparing for the winter holidays, while others wait to let the season itself generate creative ideas. Heart-warming illustrations (with many templates provided), imaginative table décor including place cards and tea-candle holders, delightful ornaments, cards, tags, and boxes offer festive, imaginative ideas for celebrating the holidays with style.

NATHALIE MÉTIVIER

[Above] A subtle winter palette of mid-toned blue, gray, and tan. An assembly of distinctively layered and curled silhouetted flowers surround a simple bowl of silver balls creating a gracious winter table or sideboard arrangement. Each paper flower consists of three stamped and silhouetted flower shapes—two large flowers with one smaller flower between them.

86

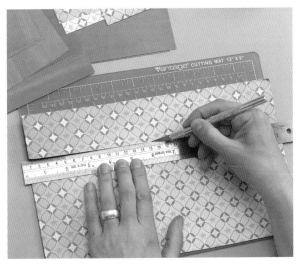

[Above, left] *Cut several (four or more) different two-sided decorative papers into manageable sized pieces.* [Above, right] *Stamp as many images in black ink on various decorative papers as needed for your arrangement, alternating colors and patterns with each flower for a unique finishing touch.*

[Above, left] *Silhouette each stamped flower shape.* [Above, right] *Create a deep recessed center in the top flower by pressing the petals up along the sides of a pencil held straight up in the center of the flower. Roll the petals of the smaller—middle—flower around a skewer to make a tight curl. Either side of the paper can face up. Keep the bottom flower flat. Attach the three flowers with a small brad through the center. Wrap together the stems of the top and middle flower with a thin strip of clear tape to accentuate the height.*

estive flower pots made with Tootsie Pops are charming place cards or party favors. Here, one is handsomely garbed in brown cardstock and the other dressed to the nines in elegant gift paper. Use the template on page 124 for this project. For each pot of flowers, punch four poinsettias from red cardstock, two facing right side up and two right side down. Cut ¼ inch down between the petals and pinch all the petals forward from the top point to add dimension. Add gold Stickles at the center of each flower. Attach the flowers at their centers, rotating each layer slightly to reveal the petals of the previous layer. Place the top two flowers facing forward and the back two facing away so the arrangement is "finished" when viewed from all sides. The upside-down lollipop stick, colored with a green pen, provides the stem for the flower, while its edible head tucked inside the pot stabilizes the structure. A holiday bow decorates the front of each pot.

JUDY RITCHIE

88

JAN WILLIAMS

[Above] Inexpensive household items can be upgraded with imaginative handmade decorations. Short glass candle holders are wrapped with a narrow gold organdy ribbon at the front of which rests a small bouquet of three quilled roses and punched leaves. See the instructions on page 118 for quilling the roses.

A strong, elegant palette of deep rose, navy blue, and white supports the simple stamped menorah image, opposite. Stamp the images twice, and silhouette the center square panel of one of the images. Color the stamped images with ink or colored pencil. Center the silhouetted square on a white cardstock mat about ½ inch larger, adding texture by popping the silhouetted square from the surface with foam mounting tape. The bold navy blue and white polka dot ribbon running from top to bottom at the center of the card front draws us immediately to the focal point. The simple all-blue palette of the stamped and layered patterned menorah at left engages us in a less formal style.

IRENE SEIFER

90

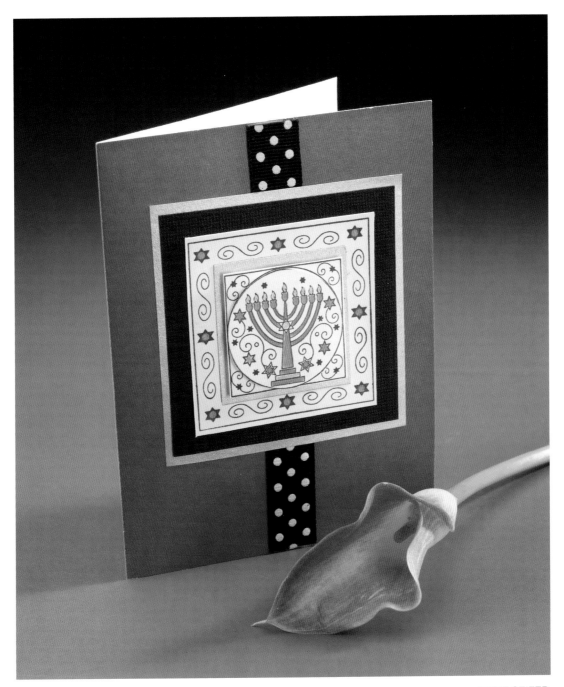

IRENE SEIFER

Happy Chanukkah

SUSAN SWAN

A menorah in the open window of a faintly visible house, opposite, beckons. Open the card to reveal a close-up of the menorah emerging from a black background wakening to the dawn of a blue sky at right. The words "Happy Chanukah" in multicolored vintage script letters were created from the same printed papers as the menorah. The papers are seen at right. This project is here to showcase the creativity of one extraordinary illustrator, for us to appreciate her imaginative approach. Wouldn't you love to receive a card from Susan?

SUSAN SWAN

onderful flat-bottomed, small glass ornaments offer two creative possibilities: they function as lovely table-top place cards when fitted with name cards, or as tree ornaments with a ribbon slipped through the top loops. Glitter snowflake designs are further embellished with quilled flowers and tight coils. See page 119 for some basic quilled shapes.

JAN WILLIAMS

SUSAN SHEPPARD

[Above] Two joyous box dolls, one dressed for Chanukah and one dressed for Christmas, perch on a mantle with accordion-folded arms holding tiny wrapped gifts, ribbon legs dangling, and tiny bell feet swaying. These disarming ornaments were created by a paper crafter with a delightful sensibility. The bodies are made with small jewelry item gift boxes standing on end; legs are blue or red ribbon strands, feet are small bells; heads are stamped on a cardstock panel that attaches to and extends down the backs of the figures.

Another colorful cut-paper illustration, below, with a child's favorite winter icon, a snowman, uses as many punched circles as possible—snowman eyes and buttons, the boy's cheeks, buttons, and hat pom-pom. The cut paper shapes are adhered to a snowy-looking light blue paper with mini white polka dots. See page 125 for a template for the snowman and friend. Have fun, and experiment with your own palette. Remember that you can adjust the template for any size you want, creating cards, tags, wrapped gifts, or even a series of book plates for a lucky younger member of the family. See the magnets we made with another illustration on page 99.

It's winter!

ROBERT CAROLA

ROBERT CAROLA

[Above] Charming, colorful cut-paper illustrations, appealing to both children and adults, adorn four sides of a simple white cube gift box. White gauze snow and a standing Christmas tree—a detail from the illustration—sit at the top. Appealing giftwrap, guaranteed to bring smiles along with a new life as a keepsake box. See the template on page 125 to create the winter bugler.

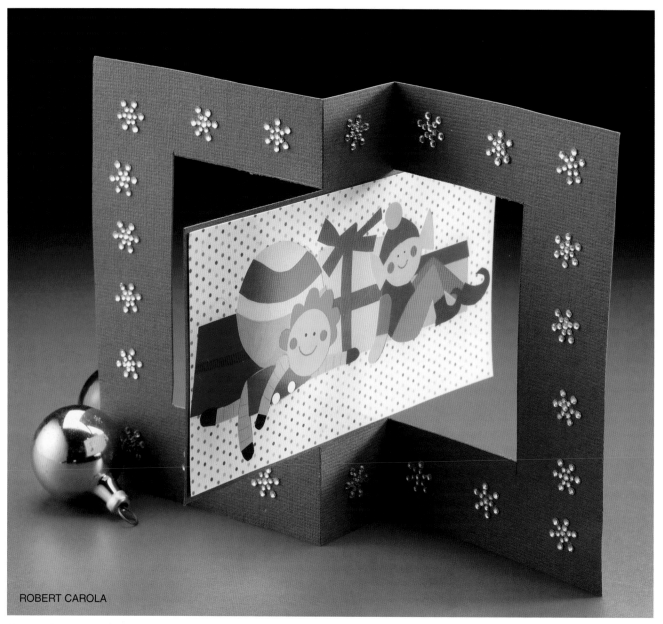

ROBERT CAROLA

[Above] A single pleated card offers a rotating window that swivels as the card is opened. The featured image is a colorful cut-paper illustration of Raggedy Ann and a Christmas elf at rest on a multicolored polka-dot field. This magical card is easy to make. See the folding template on page 125. The border around an interior cut rectangle is folded with a one-inch pleat. The swinging, cut rectangle is left attached top and bottom across the one-inch pleat. Snowflake stickers embellish the borders.

Two adorable red-cheeked youngsters carol their way into our hearts. Drawings for the figures are on page 124. Be creative. Dress the little songsters your own way, with your own palette, or use ours as a guide. The falling snow is made with lots of tiny circles punched from white cardstock, in a few sizes for variation. You can make the figures any size appropriate for your project. We made some variations for the small refrigerator magnets at left—perfect stocking stuffers or small gifts. Notice that images can be full-sized or cropped. Be imaginative: see beyond the box!

On the first day of Christmas...

ROBERT CAROLA

99

streamlined silver metal box with a full-sized Santa Claus illustration decking the top is delightful giftwrap for any age recipient. See the template on page 125 for Santa and his gifts. The same candy-cane-holding elf from the card opposite makes a charming gift tag to hang over the top of the box.

ROBERT CAROLA

ROBERT CAROLA

[Above] A red-cheeked little elf with a tricornered hat complete with pom-poms hides a candy cane behind his back rather than give it up. This little fellow can be appropriately sized for tags, cards, place cards, and other holiday decorations. See page 123 for a template. Why not make an elf bookmark with the book you give this season. That will inspire the reader to think of you and remember the holiday whenever he or she reads the book. Extend the ideas and the materials you have. Have fun.

A bright red envelope embellished with a real button; a wonderful snowman with stocking cap, chirping bird, and more real buttons tell us that it's time to celebrate. Cheerful cut colored-paper letterforms spell out "Happy Holidays." The illustration was created in Adobe Photoshop, as was the card, making it possible to print out as many cards as needed whenever they were needed.

SUSAN SWAN

JUDY RITCHIE

[Above] This trio of lighthearted holiday cards is all about layers and texture. All are simple compositions with a seasonal palette. A glittering stamped, embellished, and silhouetted snowman smiling broadly in a tidy hat and sweater takes centerstage on one card, while Christmas stockings and tree ornaments are featured on the others. All focal points are lifted from the surfaces of their cards—a delightful touch.

[Above, left] Draw the image using the template on page 124. Label each section of the drawing for color. You can assemble the cut-paper directly on your drawing. [Above, right] Select your papers to cut. It's always a good idea to lay the papers next to each other to confirm that the colors work well together. Not all reds or browns are the same.

[Above, left] Cut the shapes from the colored paper. A quick tip: trace the image onto vellum or another very light paper. Place the vellum sheet with the drawing face down on the paper to be cut. Redraw the image over the lines on the vellum. Remove the vellum and cut on the slightly indented lines. [Above, right] Layer the cut-colored paper shapes directly onto the drawing. This will give you a solid color, one-piece backing. Add finishing details—nose, button, inside ears. Silhouette the drawing.

ROBERT CAROLA

[Above] Make it small from lightweight chipboard and it's a cut-paper ornament. Make it a little larger out of various cardstock and it's a tag, or a place card. Larger still and it's a card, or a gift box topper. The possibilities are limited only by your imagination.

An unusual gift box shape, below, is decked out on two sides with layered panels featuring a stamped evergreen tree with a small star charm at the top. Wide sheer white dotted ribbon ties around the unlidded box, then through two small holes cut into the red-glittered top of the box. Experiment with variations as you create projects. It would be a fine package with the ribbon wrapped around the lidded box, but it's fun to try a new technique to create a new look. Try it this way: wrap the ribbon around the box base, cut two small holes in the box lid. Insert one ribbon end in each cut hole, place the lid on the box, and pull the ribbon through the holes to tie a graceful bow.

JAMIE KILMARTIN

106

[Above] All three festive holiday boxes were made with the templates (the box caps are separate pieces to sit on top and/or bottom) on page 126. Embellishments, papers, and some details change, but the box struc-ture remains the same. The box at left rear offers a clear window plastic middle through which the scrumptious holiday candy is visible. Seasonal papers, ribbons, and tags star.

JAN WILLIAMS

[Above] The elegant glass ornament at front is embellished with an ivory quilled snowflake constructed with loose glued coils, teardrops, marquises, open hearts shapes found on page 119. An additional C-shape coil is used—two loose coils, one at either end of a C-shape strip of quilling paper. A crystal gem nestles near center. Before attaching the quilled shapes to glass, cover the glass with glitter spray to provide a rough surface on which to glue. For this snowflake, glue six center marquise shapes together first, and build out. Assemble the complete snowflake and attach it to the glass or build the snowflake on the sprayed glass. The round glass ornament in the rear is embellished with a dramatic dark quilled snowflake.

108

Gold stars and gold twine embellish a seasonal package. The freestanding, star-punched, chocolate-filled Christmas tree place card would please any diner at a festive table. Use the template on page 126 for this simple, effective project. Buy special chocolates to hide in the base! The silver star ornament is made by punching six large stars from heavy silver cardstock. Fold each star in half vertically. Adhere the left back side of one star to the right back side of another and continue constructing in this way to form a complete six-sided star. Attach the first and last arms of the constructed star together, bringing them around in a circle. Add a silver hanging cord and a red ribbon bow. Add glue and glitter to the edges of the star as a finishing detail (or to mask any misalignments).

JUDY RITCHIE

109

*G*ift tags and more gift tags! An easy way to be creative for the holiday season. Stamping, punching, and layering prevail here. Some of our tags are literal tag shapes, others are variations. Simple as they are, each has an unexpected delightful touch. The surprise punched border reveals the red mat under the green tree stamped tag, below; a punched snowman, above, dons a dimensional red thread scarf and hat band, brad buttons and eyes, and punched snow; and a punched gingerbread man is decked out with shiny brad buttons. Those little touches do make a difference.

110

WE GATHER TOGETHER TO WISH YOU
MERRY CHRISTMAS AND HAPPY NEW YEAR

Happy Holidays

ROBERT CAROLA

[Above] Whimsical illustrations such as this trio of cards warm our hearts and make our spirits soar. And what better time of the year for warm hearts and soaring spirits than Christmas and New Year's?

111

JAN WILLIAMS

[Above] A styrofoam dome (half of a 4-inch styrofoam ball) on top of a package is covered with dozens of tiny, quilled green holly leaves and red berries interspersed with punched cardstock leaves complete with hand-drawn veins. This dedicated paper crafter has designed a beautiful package that in itself is a holiday decoration. To create a similar look, adhere quilled and punched shapes starting at the top of the dome and work down covering the whole dome. Instructions for basic quilled shapes are on page 119.

112

The holly leaves, opposite, are quilled coils. Flatten and grasp the coils in the center with tweezers. Push back on each end of the flattened coil to make three points at each end. Open the shape up to a holly leaf. The berries are loose-glued coils. Red gems and gold glitter spray used judiciously catch the light. The pleated ribbon skirt beneath the dome is just right. Right, a delicate display of tiny quilled roses in purple and white edged in silver and punched green leaves adorn the silver ribbon wrapped around and crossed at the front of two small glass tea-light holders. Instructions for quilling roses are on page 118.

JAN WILLIAMS

113

NATHALIE MÉTIVIER

[Above] Rich red and gold ornaments and intriguing place cards are sophisticated and inspiring. The ornaments are simple, commercially purchased red and gold, small- and medium-sized glass balls decorated in style with red or gold Peel Off's. Sometimes the gold Peel Off's are colored with a red Peel Off's marker. The place cards are created with modified small votive candle holders.

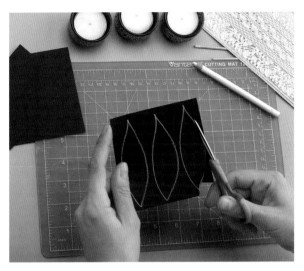

[Above, left] Remove the wick from the wax candles. Paint the small wood skewers with gold paint. Decorate the mini votive candle holders with gold Peel Off's. Draw or trace a simple leaf shape on black cardstock, and silhouette. [Above, right] Put Peel Off's leaves on black cardstock and on gold metallic paper. Color some parts of the leaves on the gold paper with a red Peel Off's marker.

[Above, left] Silhouette the Peel Off's flowers on black cardstock. Curl the leaves lightly with the blade of a pair of scissors. [Above, right] Write a guest's name on each silhouetted black leaf. Roll a glue dot around the skewer and attach the black leaf, the red and gold leaf, and the matted transparent flower to the glue dot. Cover any visible part of the glue dot with a small black cardstock strip. Insert the skewer into the wax candle.

alentine's Day is time to let your romantic nature step forward. Here is a medley of cards for this special day, each one prettier than the next. Below, a winter tree is bare except for twenty-four tiny red hearts. The layers are lovely and the off-center design is simple and pleasing. An open red heart with tiny silver hearts wafting out says everything. Two more valentines, opposite, offer similar feelings with a different palette. Color can be bright or even raucous, or unexpectedly quiet and reserved, just as texture can be obvious or subtle. It is magical when the two elements work together. The torn edge of the central panel of the gray card adds soft texture to the understated palette. The plum-colored stamped heart flowers stretching from the stamped vase offers an enchanting palette. Color does offer its own narrative style.

JUDY RITCHIE

JUDY RITCHIE

TEMPLATES

Enlarge or reduce the images as appropriate for your projects.

QUILLED ROSES, page 21

Hold the quilling tool perpendicular in the right hand. Thread the quilling paper onto tool from the left side, with the paper horizontal to the tool. Roll the paper towards the left until you have made 1½ complete turns around the tool.

Making your first fold: With the left hand, fold the paper down towards your body. The quilling paper should now be perpendicular against the tool, both going in the same direction.

Hold the paper firmly in the left hand and rotate your right arm up while holding the tool. This should make the paper form a "cone" shape on the end of the tool. Bring your right arm back down making sure to keep the

"cone" shape. For the rest of the folds: Repeat the same instructions used for the first fold until you are at the end of your strip

of paper. Generally 3inches of paper will yield 7-9 folds.

Final forming of rose: Remove your folded rose from the tool. Using a pair of pointed tweezers, hold the very center of the rose & gently turn the paper outward, the opposite way you originally folded the paper. This opens up the rose slightly. Gently fold the petals of the rose

down by grabbing several layers of folds with the tweezers and pulling them down away from the center of the rose. The "crushed" look actually does come from gently "smashing" the rose between two fingers before gluing it into place.

LEPRECHAUN, page 14

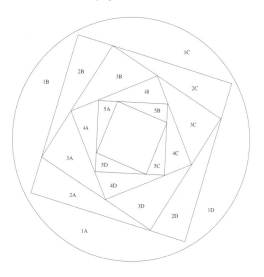

IRIS FOLD, page 38

Quilling shapes and instructions by Jan Williams.

118

SOME BASIC QUILLED SHAPES

LOOSE GLUED COIL

Roll the paper on the quilling tool to form a coil. Remove the coil from the tool. Allow the coil to relax and expand to desired size, and apply small amount of glue to the end of paper strip, gluing down to the coil.

TIGHT COIL

Roll the paper on the quilling tool to form a coil. DO NOT allow the coil to relax and expand. While the coil is still on the tool, apply small amount of glue to the end of paper strip, gluing down to the coil. Gently remove the coil from tool.

TEAR DROP

Make a loose glued coil. Pinch at one end of the coil to form a teardrop shape.

SHAPED MARQUISE

Make a marquise. Run your fingernail toward one point curling it up. Repeat at the other end curling in the opposite direction.

MARQUISE

Make a loose glued coil. Pinch at the exact opposite side of coil to form points at both ends, forming a marquise shape.

OPEN HEART

Fold a piece of paper in half. Rolling towards the center-fold, roll each end of paper inward toward the center-fold.

SHAPED TEARDROP

Make a teardrop. Run your fingernail toward the point curling the point in one direction.

SQUARE

Make a loose glued coil. Flatten the coil between your fingers. Hold the flattened coil upright between thumb and index finger with the points at the top and bottom. Flatten again matching up the previous 2 folds created by the points. Reopen to form a square shape.

HALF CIRCLE

Make a loose glued coil. Flatten one side of the coil by pinching the circle at two points or flatten coil gently against your finger.

HOLLY LEAF

Make a loose glued coil. Flatten the coil between your fingers. Hold the flattened coil in the center tightly with tweezers. Gently push one end towards center with index finger and thumb forming 2 more points. Repeat on opposite end. Reshape leaf as needed.

ROLLED HEART (ARROW)

Make a teardrop. Hold the teardrop shape between the thumb and index finger of one hand. Gently push the center of rounded end back using the straight edge of the tweezers. Crease at both sides of the pushed-in end.

CRESCENT

Make a teardrop. Pinch one more point not quite opposite of the first point. Run your fingernail toward both points curling the points up or make a loose glued coil. Press coil against the rounded side of the quilling tool or finger to give the coil a crescent shape.

119

BUTTERFLY FRAME, page 24

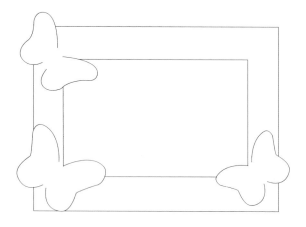

ENVELOPE CLOSURE, page 31

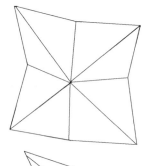

1. Fold, crease, and unfold a square of paper in half horizontally, vertically, diagonally both ways. Crease and unfold each time.

2. Squash in the sides.

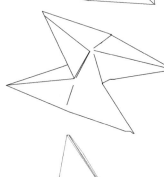

3. You will now have a triangle.

VASE FOLD, page 26

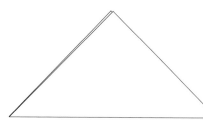

1. Fold a square piece of paper on the diagonal.

2. Turn paper so the point is at the top.

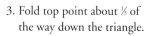

3. Fold top point about ⅓ of the way down the triangle.

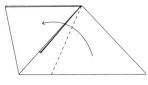

4. Fold lower left point to upper right, forming a straight line across the top.

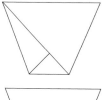

5. Fold lower right point to upper left.

6. Turn over.

120

DIAMOND TEA-BAG FOLD, page 45

GIFT CARD BOX, page 37

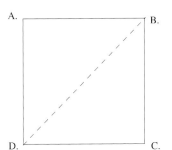

1. Fold a square of
   paper in half diag-
   onally. Crease and
   unfold.

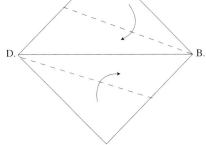

2. Rotate square 45 degrees so point A is at the
   top. Fold the A-B side in to center. Fold the
   C-D side in to center.

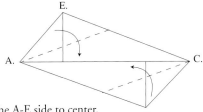

3. Fold the A-E side to center.
   Fold the C-F side to center.

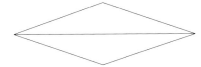

4. Turn over.

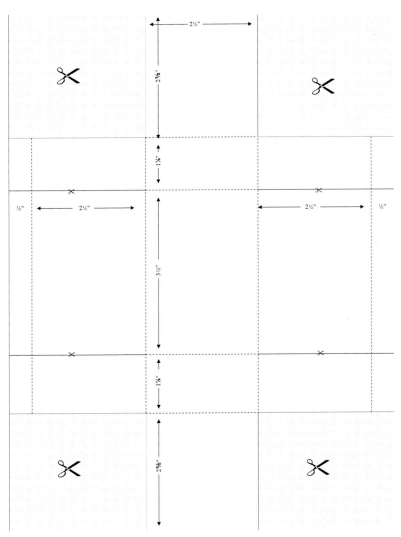

PINWHEEL, page 46

LEAF SHAPES, page 48

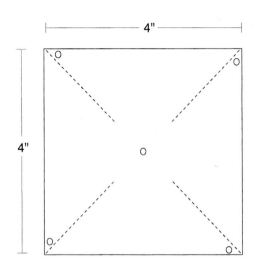

4"

4"

FLIP-TOP BAG, page 53

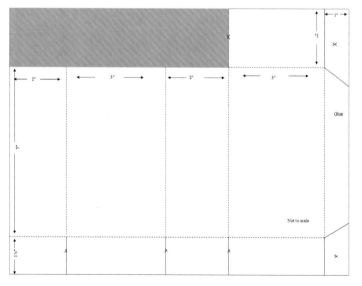

1"

2"

2"   3"   2"   3"

5"

Glue

Not to scale

1½"

Susan Swan

RIBBON EMBROIDERY GRID, page 56

STAR-SQUARE FOLD, page 55

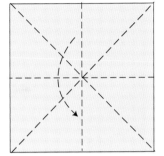

1. Fold, crease, and unfold a square of paper in half horizontally, vertically, diagonally both ways. Crease and unfold each time.

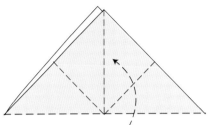

2. Turn paper with point up.

MONSTER, page 72

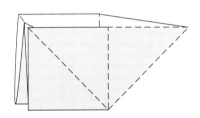

3. Squash the left triangle tip behind the front square. Squash the right triangle tip behind the square.

4. Flatten the square with point up and 2 layers on each side.

ELF, page 101

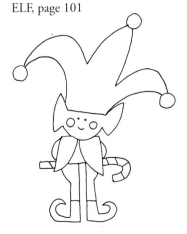

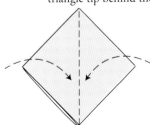

5. Fold the top layer on each side behind the top layer, in to the center.

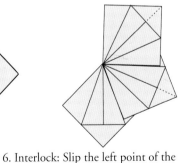

6. Interlock: Slip the left point of the bottom layer of one piece under the top layer of another; repeat with all folded diamonds. Dot glue in folds to secure.

SIMPLE POP-UP CARD, page 74

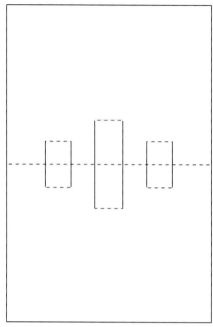

Cut on solid lines, fold on dotted lines.

FLOWER-POP POT, page 88

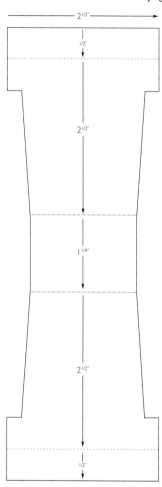

1. Score where indicated.
2. Fold the top edges in.
3. Color the stick of the lollipop with green ink, or wrap with green ribbon.
4. Tape the front to the back, sandwiching the lollipop stick between. (Stabilize the lollipop with a small piece of double-sided tape.)
5. Attach the rim pieces to the front and back to add dimension.

STOCKING WITH BEAR, page 105

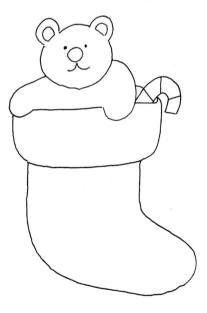

CAROLERS, page 99

SNOWMAN AND FRIEND, page 96

BUGLER, page 99

SANTA, page 100

SWIVEL CARD, page 98

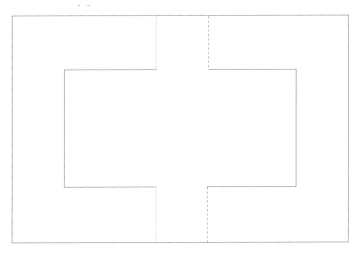

Mountain fold on the 2 short dotted lines at the left of center, and valley fold on the 2 dashed lines at the right. Cut on straight lines.

TURKEY, page 81

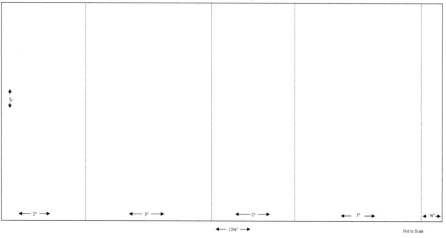

CHRISTMAS CANDY HOLDER, page 108

Cut on dashed lines.

HOLIDAY BOX, page 107

← 2" →   ← 3" →   ← 2" →   ← 3" →   ← ½" →

← 10½" →

Not to Scale

Boxes courtesy Judy Ritchie.

HOLIDAY BOX CAPS, page 107

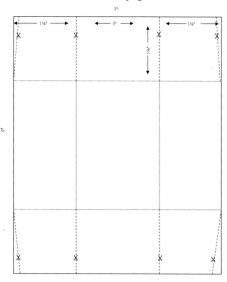

5"

← 1½" →   ← 3" →   ← 1½" →

ILLUSTRATED GLOSSARY

ACCORDION FOLDING is a succession of alternating mountain and valley folds across the surface of a card, tag, or other paper surface. You can make small booklets or decorative embellishments with an extended series of accordion folds. See page 30.

COLLAGE is a collection of artfully arranged images, papers, or other materials pasted together on a page or paper-covered object. See page 65.

CUT-PAPER ARTWORK is a technique of cutting and layering small pieces of paper or the card or tag itself to create images with color, texture, and depth. See page 72.

GATE FOLDING places the opening of a card at the center so that you can open both sides, like a gate, to reveal the interior. See page 28.

IRIS FOLDING involves arranging small cut strips of paper in a spiral pattern around a central opening, similar to the iris of the eye or lens of a camera. See page 39.

MASKING is the process of covering an image or the area around an image with fresh paper so that a second image can be stamped behind the first without covering any of the first image. Removing the mask reveals the second image in the background. See page 16.

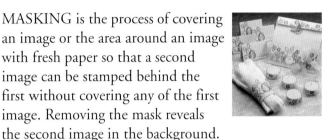

ORIGAMI is the traditional Japanese art of folding paper into representational shapes. See page 26.

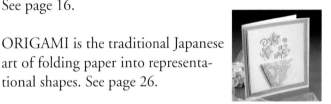

PAPER CONSTRUCTION involves building three-dimensional forms with paper and other embellishing materials. See page 94.

POP-UP CONSTRUCTION is the art of cutting, folding, and mounting an image on a card so that when you open the card the design literally pops up from the inside. See page 75.

PUNCH ART is the process of cutting shapes from paper with a hand-held punch and either using the shapes alone or combining several shapes to create new, dimensional images. Both the positive and negative shapes can be useful. See page 67.

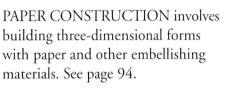

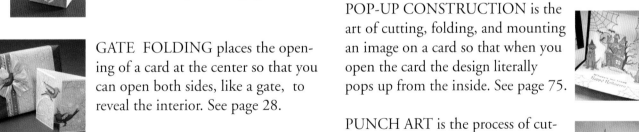

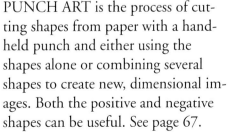

QUILLING, also called paper filigree or scroll work, is a simple decorative technique accomplished by rolling thin strips of paper around a slotted or needle tool into various shapes and then arranging and combining the shapes to embellish a design. See page 109.

TEA-BAG FOLDING, similar to origami, is the technique of folding small squares of colorful papers into interesting geometric shapes that are artfully arranged in a pleasing pattern. It is sometimes called kaleidoscope folding. See page 44.

SPIRELLI, or string art, is the art of creating linear geometric patterns of different color threads to embellish a design. See page 12.

TORN PAPER adds an intriguing, soft, undulating edge to a paper shape bringing grace, texture, and depth to a project. See page 117.

STEPPED ACCORDION FOLDING is created by changing the width or height of folded panels. It adds interest and detail to the card or tag. See page 45.

WINDOW CARDS are created by cutting appropriate-sized openings in one or more panels of a folded card, to reveal artwork visible through the cut opening. See page 39.

SWIVEL WINDOW CARDS are created by cutting a partially attached opening in a card. The cut window panel rotates, or turns, as the card is opened, revealing a new image on the rotating panel. See page 98.